The Advanced Rhyming Dictionary

Multisyllabic Rhymes for Rappers and Poets

Adam 'Shuffle T' Woollard
and
Jamie 'Bleez' Blackmore

Grosvenor House
Publishing Limited

This book is published by
Grosvenor House Publishing Ltd
Link House
140 The Broadway, Tolworth, Surrey, KT6 7HT.
www.grosvenorhousepublishing.co.uk

Produced in conjunction with
Solipsus Creative Limited

A CIP record for this book
is available from the British Library

ISBN 978-1-78623-668-5

Adam would like to dedicate this book to:
Al 'Bender' Buchannan, Pete Cashmore, Mum, Dad,
Edward, Darcey, William, Charlie, Jude and Ellen.

Jamie would like to dedicate this book to:
His family, David Kimbangi, and every girlfriend
he's bored to death for putting up with his non-stop
rhyming for 10 years.

Below is the list of people who have contributed one or more accepted suggestions to any of the various rhyme schemes in this book.

Theo 'Marlo' Marlow

Frankie 'Phraser' Speirs

Charlie 'GC' Speirs

Stuart 'Ambi' Moss

Jordan 'Olde English' English

Christ 'Twist' Taylor

Liam 'Body' Bagnall

Jack Howarth

James 'Quill' Lambert

Jed 'Soul' Mitchell

Rowan 'Eurgh' Faife

Freddie 'Cruger' Scott-Miller

Harry 'Heretic' Robinson

Santi 'Flex Digits' Perez

Seano Mac

Danny 'Craft D' Pandolfi

Stephen McCann

Sam 'Arkaic' Shaw

Harry Rae (née Baker)

Dean 'Danny Jaqq' Holder

Jeozif Haduk

Gary Osborne

Adam 'Mos Prob' Felman

Paul 'Deffinition' Tweddle

Gavin Whitby-Lear

George 'Enigma' Kelly

Tom Kwei

Pedro King

Steven Oshea

Luke 'Impact' Samuel

David Grimaldi

Tony 'D' Hamlet

Dom 'Dotz' Fletcher

Jake Hughes

Jacob Birkinshaw

Introduction

Thank you for buying this book. It's the culmination of more than seven years' solid work. Finally seeing it in physical form is incredible.

I have had a huge amount of help from an amazing circle of friends. Overleaf is a comprehensive list of all the people who have contributed to the book; look up their music, battle raps and poetry, and I'm sure you will see why I admire them so much.

But none have contributed more than my co-author Jamie 'Bleez' Blackmore, who I met in Brighton in 2014. Jamie has an incomparable ear for rhymes and without his help this book would not have been possible.

Multisyllabic rhymes can take over your life. They are insanely addictive, and they've been a constant obsession of mine for nearly a decade. This project has taken a huge amount of time and effort to complete, but it has all been worth it to develop the first multisyllabic rhyming dictionary.

I hope that you will share my passion for rhymes and use this as a reference book, a workbook and, by using the game element within the dictionary, a fun exercise book. Add your own rhymes to it and come up with amazing material; I want the book to act as a catalyst to kick-start your own creative process.

What are multisyllabic rhymes?

Unlike traditional single-syllable rhyme schemes, where just the end of the word or phrase rhymes, multisyllabic rhymes use more than one of the syllables in the word or phrase to make a longer-sounding rhyme.

This dictionary includes both two- and three-syllable rhyme schemes. The rhyming syllables we are interested in are the 'stressed' syllables.

Both syllables are stressed in the book's two-syllable words. For instance, in the band name '**PINK FLOYD**', both syllables must be rhymed and there are no unstressed syllables. Other examples include laptop/roadworks/Fight Club/hip flask.

The dictionary doesn't include schemes on words such as table/heaven/sabre/gammon (unless they are used with other words to create a longer-rhyme scheme, like 'gammon steak'), because they only have one stressed syllable followed by an unstressed syllable, and can be found in many traditional rhyming dictionaries (known as double rhymes, where there is only one stressed syllable).

When it comes to the three-syllable rhyme schemes used in this book, we only have two *stressed* syllables (the first and last), with an unstressed syllable in the middle. For example, in the phrase 'writer's room' the first and last syllables are stressed, as shown here in bold: '**WRI**ter's **ROOM**'. The second (middle) syllable doesn't really have a vowel sound in the same way: it's a 'schwa'. Other examples are aqueduct/belly laugh/cavalier/battle rap. We almost skip over the middle syllable because it is unstressed. There are no words or phrases like volcano/hard worker/train journey/John Lennon, because they don't follow the 'stressed-unstressed-stressed' pattern.

Why aren't the rhymes perfect?

When we perform rhymes like this, we are *less* focused on 'perfect rhymes', where not only the assonance or 'vowel sound' rhymes, but the consonance, too. When we perform multisyllabic rhymes, there is an inherent rhythm to them, which means that this perfection is not needed as much for it to sound pleasant. Therefore, the rhymes are not presented in alphabetical order but in a sound progression depending on how well the phrases and sounds work together.

Take 'stunt car' and 'love heart' as examples: these are multisyllabic rhymes because the assonance rhymes – UH-AR. 'Love' would not traditionally rhyme with 'stunt', and 'car' does not perfectly rhyme with 'heart'. However, when we read them aloud – 'Stunt car/love heart/tongue bar/junk yard' – we can hear the inherent rhythm carried through the vowel sounds, allowing the words to 'SLANT' OR 'HALF'-rhyme together (this is especially forgiving when heard at the end of a line, as in a traditional rap or poem).

Vowel sounds

There are only so many combinations of sounds you can have for the two-syllable and three-syllable schemes. As I see it, there are 18 vowel sounds in the sense we are talking about, shown here (I have tried to represent the sound of each one on the left, as found in the index):

A – as in Babe.
AH – as in Cat.
AR – as in Car.
AIR – as in Hair.
E – as in Speed.

EH – as in Bed.
ER – as in Burn.
EAR – as in Fear.
I – as in Lie.
IH – as in Kid.
O – as in Snow.
OH – as in God.
OR – as in Lord.
OW – as in Cow.
OOH – as in Look or Could.
OI – as in Toy.
U – as in Broom or Flu.
UH – as in Bug.

The index

Using the index in this book should be quite straightforward, but just in case, here is some information on how to use it.

It was designed to be as intuitive as possible so that you don't have to search for a particular word to rhyme with, just the sound itself. Say you come up against the rhyme 'missing man': you have writer's block but you want to keep going, so you look to your multisyllabic rhyme dictionary. You don't search for 'missing man' because it might not even be in the book; after all, it's just two words you put together out of all the word combinations you could have chosen. Instead you search for the sounds.

In this case you look for 'IH-AH' as in the vowel sounds you find in '**MISS**ing **MAN**', since, as explained above, the middle syllables are unstressed for the three-syllable schemes we use in this book. Thus, you would go to the back of the book and look for the first sound: 'IH' (the sounds in the index are in alphabetical order of the vowel).

Then you would look down the 'IH' sounds, of which there are 18, and find the corresponding second sound: 'AH'. 'IH-AH', will have a page number next to it and when you turn to that page, you will see the rhyme scheme 'IH-AH' for two syllables: 'six pack/Big Mac/KitKat' and three syllables: 'Instagram/piggyback/gingersnap'.

Accents

The book attempts to cater for as many accents as possible. If you are from some areas of north England, for example, some sounds overlap, specifically the 'OOH' as in 'wood' and 'UH' as in 'BUG'.

One of the rhymes for 'South Park' is 'OutKast', as in the band. If you are from north England, North America or countless other places, you will pronounce 'OutKast' not as 'OW-AR' but as 'OW-AH', so that it rhymes with 'mouse trap' or 'housecat'. This was one of the biggest issues with the book and how to fix it haunted me for a long time. Then my girlfriend suggested a very elegant solution, which you will see used when you get to the first 'AR' rhyme scheme that contains such an example.

Effectively, when you see that there is a discrepancy between the scheme and how *you* say the scheme, there will be a note that redirects you to the page that has the scheme as *you* would pronounce it. For example, for the words ''OutKast/houseplant and downdraft' there is a note underneath the group which tells you to turn to the page where the scheme will continue with 'outback/mouse trap/housecat', etc., because you will pronounce it as either 'Out-karst' or 'Out-Kast' (the latter like 'mass'). So, even if your accent is not the same as the writer's, you will still be able to find the rhyme scheme you're looking for.

Bear in mind, though, that this is a dictionary written mainly by two Brits, so a lot of the references will be Anglo-centric. However, we have included celebrities from both sides of the pond as well as locations, so hopefully that won't be too much of an issue.

What is and isn't included

The rhyming suggestions included in this book are words, phrases or terms that are in common parlance. They include celebrity names, place names, idioms, film titles, and so on. If it's deemed significant enough to be known by *most* people, it'll stay in. It is true that this book caters slightly more for a British audience, but that does not stop there being plenty of references to the Americas and other nations.

For example, we have 'South Park', because most people are aware of the show. We also have 'cow shark' which, it turns out, is a species of shark (a bit obscure, but it wasn't the easiest rhyme scheme). There's also 'clown car', which draws to our imagination the clown's car that holds an impossible number of people, which has become an idea most are familiar with.

We haven't wasted time by adding suggestions that aren't self-contained ideas. For example, in the scheme 'OW-AR' we don't have suggestions like 'loud bark', which is just an adjective next to a noun or 'brown mark' which is a vague, non-concrete idea. If we had included these there would have been an infinite combination of words we *could* also have added.

And what this book is *not* designed to be is a collection of obscure words you have to look up in a separate dictionary or online. For example, you won't often find obscure mythological references, scientific names of diseases, or mathematical terms. This book is designed to be a *really* practical tool for people writing songs, hip-hop, poetry, and anything else that could employ multisyllabic rhymes that are intuitive and self-contained.

I want it to be something that will help you again and again, not something that you find a few nice rhymes in but only pick up once.

We haven't added *every* single rhyme we could think of. A lot of lists have at least 20 other rhymes that *could* have been added, but there's no point making one scheme 40 rhymes long when some more difficult schemes only have a small handful of rhymes, or none at all in some cases. This is simply because some rhyme schemes are a lot easier than others and some are very difficult. Also, this is a workbook as well as a dictionary and it is important that people can add to the schemes themselves, rather than just have 1,000 rhymes per scheme and no space to contribute.

You also will find we have included some schemes with only one rhyme; if you are writing a piece with something specific that doesn't fit into our definition of what to include, that one rhyme may be helpful to you.

Finally, a note on the letter 'L'. It seems odd, but 'L's can throw you right off a rhyme scheme. I'm not a linguist and I'm not going to look up the terms because it doesn't really matter, but the key takeaway is that 'L's can sometimes change the rhyme, depending on where they are in a word. For example, the word 'bold' only really rhymes with words that have an 'L' at, or near, the end. 'Bold' doesn't (at least in my accent; I'm sure it's different in different places) rhyme with, say, 'code' or 'zone', but it does rhyme with 'goal' and 'fold'. It has its own unique sound. But to avoid complication, I have tried (for the most part) to eliminate from the book 'L's that occur in this position. I just think it makes it simpler. Maybe I will include them in a future edition.

The multi-game

The game aspect of this book is one that I, and many of my family and friends (so they tell me), have played and enjoyed. It is also a great way to get better at clocking multisyllabic rhymes more quickly. The idea is this:

The game host (the person holding the book) starts off a rhyme scheme: 'the rhyme scheme is "handiwork"'. The other players see that the rhyme scheme as AH-ER. The host then gives clues to the players as to what the next rhyme in the book's sequence is:

'Someone who doesn't speak a lot is...'

The players will compete to be the first to answer: 'Taciturn'

'At the end of the financial year, you need to do your...'

'Tax return'

'And if there was less to pay than you'd expected you would have...'

'Cash to burn'

It's a very addictive game, especially if you have a good host who can come up with difficult clues that make it harder to guess. For an extra layer of the game, you could make the clues rhyme with the answer. What a fun way to spend your Sunday afternoons! Sudoku's boring, anyway.

And finally

I hope you enjoy this book and find it both useful and fun, and we look forward to hearing people clocking rhymes we've never thought of, and perfecting schemes and learning how to rhyme effectively. Yes indeed.

Adam (Shuffle T)

A-A	A-AH	A-AR
Payday	Placemat	Face mask
Ray J	ASAP	Stage pass
Mate's rates	Payback	Stained glass
Slave trade	Kate Nash	*See A-AH*
Face paint	Take That	Gay bar
Vacate	Rain mac	Braveheart
Freight train	Stray cat	Skate park
Waylaid	Stagehand	Trademark
Play date	Mainland	Radar
Gameplay	Haystack	Graveyard
Namesake	Age gap	Race car
James Blake		Brain fart
	Stacey Dash	
Takeaway	Paperback	Raise a glass
JFK	Maniac	Blade of grass
Labour day	Databank	*See A-AH*
David Blaine	Payment plan	Ace of hearts
Hateful 8	Bacon bap	Cable car
Mayonnaise	Dating app	Razor-sharp
Layer Cake	Change of tack	Bass guitar
Paper plane	Baby fat	Trailer park
Flava Flav	Safety mat	Change of heart
Ace of Spades	Laser tag	Maker's mark
Razorblade	Makeup bag	Playing cards
Database	Basement Jaxx	Bakewell tart

A-AIR
Day care
Train fare
Mayfair
Stray hair
Jane Eyre
Laid bare
Caged bear
Spayed mare

Facial hair
Vacant stare
Gaming chair
Say your prayers
Baby wear
Laissez faire

A-E
Baked beans
Dre Beats
Jay Z
Rapeseed
Page 3
Train seat
A-Team
Daydream
James Dean

Mainstream
Eighteen

Ancient Greece
Table read
Take a seat
A to B
Blatantly
KFC
Graham Greene
Jamie T
Bakery

A-EH
Train wreck
Caged hens
Cavemen
Wavelength
Brain dead
Safe sex
Rain check
Latex
Break bread
Straight edged
Mae West
Apex

Space cadet
Break a leg
Bated breath
Pastry chef
Grateful Dead
Bayonet
Razor edged
Sacred text
Maisonette
Safety net

A-ER
Caged bird
Face first
Brain surge
Plane curve
Framework
Pay dirt
Tapeworm

Paperwork
April 1st
Date of birth
Phrasal verb
Safety first
Racial slur
Ladybird

Facial burns
Wait your turn

A-EAR
Shakespeare
Reindeer
Ray Mears
Cape Fear
Grey beard
Cake tier

Crate of beer
Safety gear
Navy Pier
Baby deer
Play by ear
Face your fears
Cambridgeshire

A-I
FaceTime
Grapevine
Ralph Fiennes
Waistline
Hate crime
Brake light

Cage fight
Steak knife
Stage fright
Drainpipe
Layby
A.I

Sage advice
Katie Price
Baby Spice
Rachel Weisz
Dana White
David Icke
Break the ice
Naked eye
Pastry knife
Nationwide
Waste of time

A-IH
Spaceship
Matrix
Facelift
Playlist
Payslip
Saint Nick

Basics
Snake pit
Crayfish
Cake mix

Babysit
Taylor Swift
Jason Biggs
Faking it
Flaming Lips
Zadie Smith
Paperclip
Makes you
   think
Safety pin
David Lynch

A-O
Rainbow
Waistcoat
Halo
NATO
Cane toad
Scapegoat
Payload
Gravestone

K.O.
Grace Jones
J Lo
Lay low

Radio
Game of
    Thrones
HBO
Status Quo
Gravy boat
Way to go
H2O
Ancient Rome
Stately home
Shaving foam

A-OH
Raindrop
Brainwash
Stray dog
Day job
Great Scott
Jay cloth
Kate Moss
Face off
Asos

Baywatch
James Bond

Jamie Foxx
Sadie Frost
Blazing Squad
Tablecloth
Shake it off
Crazy Frog
David Cross
Tater Tots
Pagan Gods

A-OR
Skateboard
Acorn
Shane Ward
Train doors
Décor
Chainsaw
Main course
Brainstorm

Pastry fork
David Morse
Jason Bourne
Safety form

Ravenclaw
Labour laws
Trading floor
Table saw

A-OW
Lake House
Stake out
Face down
Raincloud
Playground
Greyhound
Space bound
Grace Town
James Brown

Safe and sound
Sacred grounds
Paper round
Crazy Town
Danger Mouse
Famous Grouse
Break it down
Layabout
Take me out

A-OI
Gameboy
Raised voice
James Joyce

Case in point
Paperboy
Make some
  noise
Baby toys
David Moyes

A-OOH
Facebook
Kate Bush
Dane Cook
James Woods
Stay put

Neighbourhood
Greater good
Made you look
Rachel Cook
Safety hook

A-U
Grapefruit
Babe Ruth
Debut
Breakthrough
Playroom
Stay tuned
Late bloom
HQ
Grey Goose
GameCube

Tablespoon
Sailor moon
Sabre-toothed
Naked truth
Pay your dues
Raise the roof
Bakerloo
Baby food
Breaking news
Bathing suit

A-UH
Make up
A cup

Paintbrush
BASE jump
James Blunt
Gay club
Taste buds

Paper cut
Ladybug
Break it up
Stay in touch
Hazel nut
Baby bump
Ace of clubs
Staple gun
Naked Lunch
Brady Bunch
Bay for blood
Making love

AH-A
Ashtray
Handshake
Backstage
Flatmate
Translate
Rampage

Blank slate
Flank steak
Landscape

Abdicate
Gareth Gates
Alex Zane
Matinée
Sabbath day
Kathy Bates
Shallow Grave
Camel case
Stanley blade
Masquerade
Barricade
Navigate

AH-AH
Backpack
Anthrax
Hatchback
Anne Frank
Ransacked
Jack Black
Zack Braff
Cat flap

Land mass
Taxman
Bandstand

Action packed
Jackie Chan
Transit van
Traffic jam
Parallax
Cadillac
Canvas bag
Caravan
Taliban
Anagram
Handicap
Cactus Jack

AH-AR
Lap dance
See AH-AH
Grandpa
Stan Marsh
Jam tart
Scrapyard
Ant farm
Landmark
Vanguard

Bank card
Rampart

Happenstance
Cary Grant
Avalanche
See AH-AH
Andrew Marr
Alan Carr
Camouflage
Knacker's yard
Handlebars
Catherine Parr
Abattoir
Sabotage
Strapless bra
Pack of cards

AH-AIR
Black bear
Hat hair
Cab fare
Flat share
Blank stare
Hand-care
Damp air
Flatware

Panda bear
Cancer scare
Camembert
Camping chair
Matted hair
Magic square
Active Wear

AH-E
Bad dreams
Scrap heap
Backseat
Fat free
Stampede
Vaccine
Tag team
Stan Lee
Crab tree
Plan B
Fact sheet

Handkerchief
Anne-Marie
Halloween
Janet Leigh
Japanese
Aberdeen

Trampoline
Tambourine
Tangerine
Mantelpiece
Apple tree

AH-EH
Black Death
Blank cheque
NatWest
Access
Andrex
Crash test
Flatbread
Bad breath
Grand theft

Adam West
Bangladesh
Marrakesh
Scrambled eggs
Parapets
Standing desk
Ant and Dec
Fancy dress
Baroness
Dragons Den

AH-ER
Blackbird
Slang word
Antwerp
Hamburg
Adverb
Cat fur
Bratwurst
Bag search
Trapped nerve
Patchwork
Frankfurt
Transferred

Handiwork
Taciturn
Tax return
Cash to burn
Back to work
As you were
Angry Birds
Captain Kirk
Amber Heard
Battenberg
Kathy Burke
Planet Earth
Magic words

AH-EAR
Blackbeard
Stand clear
Gap year
Cashmere
Pap smear
Hampshire
Frank Mir
Tangier
Pam Grier

Atmosphere
Chandelier
Cavalier
Rabbit ears
Bandolier
Anchor beard
Camping gear
Lancashire
Racketeer
Bank cashier

AH-I
Backside
Landslide
Anne Rice

Jack White
Magpie
Flash drive
Pad Thai
Crack pipe
Camp site
Standby
Pan fried
Cats eyes

Appetite
Apple pie
Stalagmite
Alibi
Valentine
Chat up line
Palestine
Jackson Five
Dragonfly
Tantalise
Gladys Knight
Paradise
Frankenstein
Bag for life

AH-IH
Brad Pitt
Crab stick
Blacksmith
Tactics
Bandwidth
Backflip
Sanskrit
Handpicked
Catnip
Ad-lib

Magic trick
Candlestick
Masochist
Apple pips
Arabic
Catalyst
Maggie Smith
Ann Boleyn
Sacrilege
Cannabis
Adjective
Battleship
Laxative

AH-O	AH-OH	
Rambo	Caps lock	Platform
Lactose	Laptop	Hacksaw
Lab coat	Matchbox	App Store
Django	Jack Frost	Sandstorm
Bank loan	Crackpot	Gas board
Backbone	Ascot	Gang war
Hand soap	Flash mob	Blackboard
Sandstone	Sasquatch	Crab claw
Cash flow	Shamrock	Transport
Chat show	Bank job	
	Lamb chops	Paramour
Saxophone		Matador
Aled Jones		Cancer ward
Rag'n'Bone	Travis Scott	Back and forth
Tally Ho!	Apple watch	Scrabble board
Antelope	Sandwich shop	Santa Claus
Savile Row	Carriage clock	Apple sauce
Sharon Stone	Carrot top	Astronaut
Amber Rose	Macintosh	Capricorn
Camel toe	Act of God	
Anecdote	Paradox	**AH-OW**
Paddleboat	Hasselhoff	Black out
Average Joe	Magic wand	Bad crowd
		Hands down
	AH-OR	Dan Brown
	Landlord	Background
	Trap door	Crack house

Lansdowne
Stand proud
Smash mouth
Hash brown

Bank account
Paramount
Shanty town
Hand me downs
Bassett Hound
Manor House
Blabbermouth
Talent scout
Battlegrounds

AH-OI
Android
Fan boy
Cash point
Pak Choi
Sangfroid
Tabloid
Tannoy
Factoid

Adenoids
Paranoid

Saveloy
Trapezoid
Backstreet boys
Gammon joint
Anna Freud
Land, ahoy

AH-OOH
Scrap book
Canned goods
Dachshund
Manhood
Flatfoot
Fan hook

Captain Hook
Matthew
Goode
Sandalwood
Babadook
Bramble bush
Hand and foot
Ration book

AH-U
Shampoo
Lampoon

Bamboo
Brand new
Tracksuit
Chat room
Stab proof
Pan flute
Thank you
Statue
Thatched roof

Carrot juice
Carrie Coon
Parachute
Malibu
Magaluf
Kangaroo
Caribou
Snaggletooth
Shatterproof
Catacomb
Camera crew

AH-UH
Dandruff
Stand up
Manhunt
Handgun

Bankrupt
Slam dunk
Grandson
Bad luck
Packed lunch
Samsung
Fan club

Rabbit hutch
Magic touch
Daffy duck
Atlas Shrugged
Basil Brush
Aqueduct
Captain Crunch
Stanley Cup
Candy Crush

AR-A
Last place
Classmate
Pathway
See AH-A
Arcade
Barmaid
Spa break
Mark Twain

Heartache
Margate
Stargaze
Shar Pei

Basket case
Masking tape
Francis Drake
Castaway
See AH-A
Army base
Charlemagne
Harlem Shake
Marketplace
Carpet stain
Marvin Gaye
Father's Day
Marmalade
Parking space

AR-AH
Grassland
See AH-AH
Hardhat
Carjacked
Tarmac
Bra strap

Armbands
Star man

Laughing gas
See AH-AH
Army camp
Smarty pants
Stalingrad
Barking mad
Heart attack
Cardiac
Starter pack
Marzipan

AR-AR
Barn dance
StarCraft
See AR-AH
Tartar
Aardvark
Farmyard
Armed guard
Arm bar
Bar chart
Car park
Cardsharp

Masterclass
See AH-AH
Garden plant
Artist pass
See AR-AH
After dark
See AH-AR
Marble Arch
Haagen Dazs
Marks and
    Sparks
Mardi Gras
Barclaycard
Harpo Marx

AR-AIR
Plant care
See AH-AIR
March hare
Bar flare
Armchair
Car share
Dark hair
Hardware
Art Fair

Arctic hare
Car repair
Harsh but fair
Armpit hair
Charley Bear
Berkeley square
Barber's chair
Market share

AR-E
Ask Jeeves
Khaki
See AH-E
Car keys
Barkeep
Heartbeat
Sardines
Shark teeth
Marquee

Tara Reid
See AIR-E
Half asleep
Masterpiece
See AH-E
Cardi B
Harper Lee

Charlie Sheen
Harmony
Market street
Pharmacy
Pardon me

AR-EH
Past tense
Naan bread
See AH-EH
Jarhead
Park bench
Sharp edge
Far fetched
Dark red
Clark Kent
Star Trek
Arm rest

Masterchef
See AH-EH
Garden fence
Marmoset
Kanye West
Charlotte's web
Father Ted
Architect

14

Martin Kemp
Garlic bread
Marker pen

AR-ER
Password
Last nerve
Craftwork
Staff nurse
See AH-ER
Bar work
Starburst
Sharp turn
Heartburn
Larkspur
Yardbirds

Afterbirth
See AH-ER
Hard at work
Charlotte
    Church
Carpet burns
Calm your
    nerves
Parting words
Arctic birds

AR-EAR
Craft beer
Last year
See AH-EAR
Mark Beard
Farm-reared
Berkshire

Darkest fear
Derbyshire
Marketeer
Lars von Trier
Carling beer
Garden shears
Farming gear
Far and near
Hard to hear

AR-I
Brass Eye
See AH-I
Marmite
Star sign
Dart flights
Far cry
Cartwright
Shark bite

Park life
Part time
Hard drive
Bra size
Carbine

Mastermind
See AH-I
Parking fine
Father time
Scarred for life
Stars and
    Stripes
Archetype
Carpet Right
Carving knife
Starry night

AR-IH
Armpit
Starfish
Yardstick
Car sick
Hardship
Tar pit
Artist
Card tricks

Arctic
Shark fin

Francis Crick
See AH-IH
Marksmanship
Parlour trick
Artie Ziff
Gaza Strip
Narcissist
Carnal sin
Bargain bin
Carpeting

AR-O
Aunt Flo
Halftone
Bath robe
Pass code
See AH-O
Cargo
Fargo
Smart phone
Carload
Bravo
Barcode
Spark Notes

Answerphone
Afterglow
See AH-O
Artichoke
Sandra Oh
Blarney Stone
Garden gnome
Garlic clove
Parking zone
Marylebone

AR-OH
Craft shop
Plant pot
See AH-OH
Star-crossed
Arm lock
Mark Strong
Car bomb
Argon
Bar job
Heartthrob
Hardtop
Guard dog
Smart watch

Aftershock
Laughing stock
See AH-OH
Barbershop
Lara Croft
Parking lot
Charlie Sloth
Carpet shop
Starting blocks

AR-OR
Passport
Task force
Dance floor
See AH-OR
Dark horse
Dartboard
Star Wars
Art form
Hardcore
Parkour
Car door
Card fraud

Masters course
Last resort
Afterthought

See AH-OR
Charley horse
Cargo shorts
Parcelforce
Arkansas
Martial law
Martin Shaw
Argonaut
Car exhaust
Gare du Nord

AR-OW
Class clown
Dance lounge
Cast doubt
Bath house
Pass out
See AH-OW
Spa town
Dark cloud
Star bound
Fart sounds
Smart mouth

Branching out
Casting couch
See AH-OW

Market town
Card account
Charlie Brown
Party House

AR-OI
Bath toy
Blastoise
See AH-OI
Charge point
Dark soy
Arm joint
Spark joy
Farm boy

Castor Troy
Master Droid
See AH-OI
Party Boy
Almond Joy
Starting point
Calming voice

AR-OOH
Passbook
Grant Wood
See AH-OOH

Garth Brooks
Hardwood
Dartmouth

Afterwards
See AH-OOH
Fatherhood
Barbara Bush
Hardback book
Farthing Wood

AR-U
Classroom
Dance moves
Brass tubes
Fast food
Grassroots
Half moon
See AH-U
Cartoon
Shark tooth
Dark blue
Car boot
Armed troops

Afternoon
Fast and loose

Cast and crew
See AH-U
Barbecue
Marmaduke
Martin Clunes
Marvin's Room
Party food
Army boots
Charlie Puth
Harvest moon

AR-UH
Daft punk
Half cut
Bathtub
Dance club
Glass jug
See AH-UH
Starstruck
Large cup
Bar none

Aftersun
See AH-UH
Partner up
Parseltongue
Carling Cup

Party bus
Garbage truck
Bargain hunt

AIR-A
Air raid
Pear shaped
Spare change
Staircase
Scared straight
Hairspray
Clare Danes
Fair trade
Caretake

Tearaway
Mary Jane
Sarah Payne
Sharing plate
Fairy cake
Aeroplane

AIR-AH
Bear trap
Prayer mat
Share bag
Air Max

Hairband
Bareback
Pear schnapps

Parent Trap
Hairy back
Sharing pack
Bear attack
Scaredy-cat

AIR-AR
Square dance
Fair chance
Hair mask
Prayer stance
See AIR-AH
Swear jar
Spare parts
Pear tarts
Bare arse

Air guitar
Dairy farm
Mary Hart
There we are
Where to start?

18

AIR-AIR
Care bear
There, there
Airfare
Fair share
Haircare

Tear and share
Wear and tear
Fair and square

AIR-E
Carefree
Bare feet
Pear tree
Spare key
Rare meat
Hair piece
Prayer beads
Airstream
Scary

Dairylea
Carefully
Sara Lee
Where's the
   beef?

Bering Sea
Rarity
Fairy Queen

AIR-EH
Hairnet
Bare chest
Chair leg
Heiress
Airhead
Fair test
Stair set

Hairy chest
Pair of legs
There and then
Air cadet
Fairer sex

AIR-ER
Swear word
Bear fur
Rare bird

Prairie skirt

AIR-EAR
Tear here

Mary Beard

AIR-I
Airtight
Hairline
Spare time
Fair fight
Rare sight
Whereby

Scary Spice
Fairy lights
Pair of tights
Air supply
Bear in mind
Erudite
Paring knife

AIR-IH
Scared stiff
Blair Witch
Spare ribs
Air Wick
Rarebit

Hair clip
Harelip
Stair lift
Airship
Fair-skinned

Chairmanship
Aerosmith
Share a kiss
Seraphim
Swearing-in
Wearing thin

AIR-O
Aero
Scarecrow
Pharaoh
Barebones
Care home
Pear's soap
Airflow
Spare clothes

Dairy goat
There you go
Mary Rose

Share the load
Swear an oath

AIR-OH
Fair cop
Scared off
AirPods
Ayer's Rock
Pear drops
Whereof

Pair of socks
Scaring off
Fairy wand
Dairy Box
Prairie dog
Pharoahe
 Monch
Sarah Cox
Swear to God
Spare the rod

AIR-OR
Airport
Therefore
Bear claw

Rare form
Care ward

Air support
Aeronaut
Sarah Chalke
Pair of shorts
Spare a thought
Aaron Swartz

AIR-OW
Stare down
Fairground
Warehouse
Aired out

Dairy cow
Chairman Mao
Bearing down
Whereabouts
Shared account
Wear a frown

AIR-OI	**AIR-U**	**AIR-UH**
Claire Foy	Fair use	Square one
Cher Lloyd	Spare room	Air brush
Fair point	Heirloom	Hair cut
Shared voice	Pear juice	Snare drum
Yeah, boy	Hairdo	Flare gun
	Square root	Bear hug
AIR-OOH	Aircrew	
Prayer book		Fair enough
Barefoot	Mary Sue	Fairy dust
	Claire de Lune	Tear it up
Parenthood	Sarah Drew	Pair of gloves
Caring Wood	Pair of shoes	

E

E-A
Cheapskate
Speed date
Green Day
Steam train
eBay
Briefcase
Heat wave
Sweepstake
Deep space
Tea cake

Peter Kay
DNA
Secret shame
Pizza base
Streets of rage
Steeplechase
Liam Payne
Tina Fey
Rearrange
Leap of faith
Piece of cake

E-AH
Beanbag
Rematch

Green Flag
Tree sap
He-Man
Kneecap
Lee Mack
Feedback
Street act
Beeswax
Heat map

Fleetwood Mac
Celiac
Sleeping bag
Beanie hat
Secret lab
Sneak attack
Freedom act
Iain Banks
Reattached

E-AR
Freelance
Ski mask
Free pass
Street dance
See E-AH
Green card

Recharge
Tree bark
Flea dart
Sweetheart
Theme park
Queen's guards

Freedom pass
Keema naan
See E-AH
Regent's Park
Queen of hearts
Lead guitar
Evening star
Treacle tart
Chico Marx
Street bazaar

E-AIR
Seafare
Clean air
Streetwear
Beach chair
Bleached hair
Re-share
Steam fair

Legionnaire
Be prepared
Greasy hair
Evening prayer
Secret lair
Regent Square

E-E
Sea breeze
E.T
P.G
Knee deep
Sweet pea
TV
Greenpeace
Tea leaves
Cream cheese
Cheat sheet

BBC
VIP
Eazy E
DVD
G&T
Eva Green
Steve McQueen

Regent Street
Secrecy

E-EH
Seabed
Reject
Key West
Bleep test
T Rex
Steam pressed
Prefect
Street cred
Cream eggs
Beachheads

Evil dead
Pizza bread
Sleepyhead
Jesus wept
Repossessed
Easter egg
Weaker sex
Eton mess
Sea cadets

E-ER
Teamwork
Knee jerk
Research
Bean curd
Keyword
Feet first
Breech birth
Lead nurse
Reverb
Seabird
T-shirt

Needlework
Pleated skirt
Sleeveless shirt
Piece of dirt
Re-emerged
Eat your words
Keep alert

E-EAR
Treebeard
Repierced
Three cheers
Wheat beer

Keep clear
Leap year

Reappear
Steven Greer

E-I
Seaside
Street fight
Steve Vai
Green light
Knee high
Levi's
Free dive
Beehive
Streamlined
Weeknight
Cheese knife
Meantime

Stephen Fry
Jesus Christ
CSI
Redefined
Ian Wright
Tree of life
Peace of mind

Pizza slice
Pecan pie
Speed of light
Secret spy
Penalised

E-IH
Egypt
Greek myth
Free kick
Seasick
Cheese stick
Ski lift
Sheepskin
Remit
Wii fit
Gee-whiz
Steamship

Leadership
Plead the fifth
Secretive
Pianist
Hedonist
Cheesy chips
Stephen King

E-O
Dreamboat
Free throw
Cheat code
Peep show
Meatloaf
Heatstroke
Cheap joke
Heathrow
Cheekbone
Ski slope
Deep throat

Decompose
Presupposed
P&O
Peter Jones
Secret code
Weekly show
Seize the throne
Speakerphone

E-OH
Treetops
Beatbox
Steve Jobs
Screenshot

Leapfrog
Teapot
Eavesdrop
Sweet spot
Cheap shot
Sheep dog
Greek god

Peeping Tom
Sweeney Todd
Deacon Frost
Pizza box
Weekly shop
Peaks and
    troughs
ZZ Top
Beat the odds

E-OR
Keyboard
Resource
Detour
Seahorse
Seesaw
Free form
Igor
Screen door

Ouija board
Mi Amor
Secret sauce
Reassured
Keeping score
Either/or
Ethan Hawke
Venusaur
Theodore

E-OW
Treehouse
Keep out
Beansprout
Meow
Rebound
Deep South
Freetown
Beat down

Leave it out
Keep it down
Evening gown
Three's a crowd
Peter Crouch

Eating out
Reach around

E-OI
B Boy
Free choice
Deep voice
Beef joint
Key point

Re-employed
Beastie Boys
Needlepoint

E-OOH
E-book
Meat hook
Priesthood
Steam cooked
Beachwood
Eastward

Peter Cook
Oedipus
Cedar wood
Fleet of foot
Read a book

E-U	E-UH	Checkmate
Reboot	Speed bump	Headache
Emu	Green thumb	Neck brace
Sweet tooth	Tree trunk	Sensei
Pea shoot	Teacup	Wednesday
Deep blue	Ski jump	Webpage
See through	Keep up	
Keith Moon	Prenup	Lemonade
Teaspoon	Peanut	MMA
Seafood	Clean cut	Quentin Blake
Preview	Peach fuzz	Reggie Yates
Beetroot	Beachfront	Retrograde
		Jessie J
Beetlejuice	Pizza Hut	Etta James
Sweet	Ethan Hunt	Second rate
vermouth	Peking Duck	Tessellate
Scenic route	Cheesy puffs	Mental age
Pikachu	Deconstruct	Rebel base
Vegan food	Steaming drunk	Bellyache
Ps and Qs	Tweedle Dum	Pencil case
Pre-approved		Featherweight
CPU	**EH-A**	
Read the room	X-ray	**EH-AH**
Deacon Blue	Lead plate	Setback
	Bench weight	Mencap
	Sex tape	Left hand
	Chess game	Wet patch

29

Sweat rash
Death trap
Jet black
Stepdad
Meth lab
Headband
Webcam

Men in black
Terence Stamp
Weatherman
LEGOLAND®
Leg of lamb
Second hand
Petty cash
Pebbledash
Bedroom tax
Temper Trap
Treasure map

EH-AR
Steadfast
Eggplant
See EH-AH
Depth charge
Head start
Death Star

Renoir
Stretch marks
Red car
Get Smart

Lemongrass
Belly laugh
See EH-AH
Reportage
Deck of cards
Question mark
Extra large
Kevin Hart
Breakfast bar
Centre Parcs
Debit card
Seminar

EH-AIR
Fresh air
Threadbare
Menswear
Chest hair
Edgware
Death stare
Deck chair

Debonair
Fred Astaire
Delaware
Teddy bear
Everywhere
Questionnaire
Dentist chair
Well aware
Medicare
Leicester
    Square
Wedding fair

EH-E
Bed sheet
Pepsi
Jet ski
Sex scene
Dead heat
Fresh meat
Jet Li
Webbed feet
Red Sea
Pet peeve
Breastfeed

Tennessee
Seventeen
Twenty three
Therapy
Mezzanine
Meryl Streep
Seven Seas
Sexy beast
Venice Beach
Denim jeans
Neckerchief

EH-EH
Dead set
Fred West
Sex pest
Death threats
Tempest
Bed rest
Jet set
Nest egg
Best friend
Tex-Mex

Megadeth
Eminem
Second best

Special guest
Epithet
Treasure chest
Represent
Heaven sent

EH-ER
Legwork
Expert
Fred Durst
Ben Hur
Geoff Hurst
N-Word
Ed Byrnes
Sweatshirt
Headfirst
Net worth
Fenchurch

Extrovert
Chequered shirt
Leather skirt
Men at work
Red alert
Spread the
    word
Secateurs

Dental works
Leavenworth

EH-EAR
Headgear
Red beard
Becks Vier
Deaf ears
Next year
Cheshire
Yes, dear

Grenadier
Yellow Beard
Engineer
Second gear
Hemisphere
Yesteryear
Genderqueer
Brexiteer

EH-I
Website
Bedside
French fries
Penknife
Egg whites

31

Necktie
Hen night
Test drive
Head lice
Ex-wife
Sex life

Kevin Kline
Twenty nine
Question Time
Left behind
Gemini
Edgar Wright
Jeopardise
Shepherd's Pie
Wesley Snipes
Genocide
Enterprise
Cellulite

EH-IH
Netflix
Set list
Death wish
Exit
Clenched fist
Friendship

Tetris
Breath mints
French kiss
Dentist
Bed spring

Methodist
Prejudiced
Exorcist
Peppa Pig
Jellyfish
Heretic
Penmanship
Get a grip
Sedative
Twenty six
Reykjavik

EH-O
Dress code
Bedclothes
Trench coat
Headstone
French toast
Glenn Close
West Coast
Death row

Strep throat
Breaststroke
Headphones

Emma Stone
Megaphone
Terry Jones
Petticoat
Head to toe
Mexico
Eskimo
Set in stone
Telephone
Stethoscope
Episode
Xenophobe

EH-OH
Bedrock
Desktop
Leg-lock
Pen pot
Hedgehog
Red Cross
End of
Despots
Headshot

Xbox
Sweatshops
Ken Dodd
Send off

Megan Fox
Dental floss
Letterbox
Record shop
Pepper pot
Leopard spot
Jelly tots
Chesty cough
Equinox
Clever clogs
Belly flop
Eddie Brock

EH-OR
Headboard
Bedsores
Red Dwarf
French door
Export
Wet floor
Centaur
Escort

Test score
Mentor
Dreadnought

Dresser drawer
Less is more
Metaphor
Chesney Hawks
Denis Law
Demi Moore
Semaphore
Tennis court
Endomorph
Checkerboard
Menopause
Peppercorn

EH-OW
Guesthouse
Endowed
Bed bound
Step down
Checkout
Headcount

Derren Brown
Kentish Town

Wedding vows
Dressing gown
Member's
   lounge
Second round
Well endowed
Settle down
Check it out
Ezra Pound

EH-OI
Rent boy
Sex toy
Checkpoint
Exploits

Tenderloin
Pet Shop Boys
Second choice
Mechanoid
Pressure points
Celluloid
Haemorrhoids

EH-OOH
Textbook
Trench foot

Left hook
Westbrook
Wet-look
Redwood

Tenterhooks
Peckerwood
Kelly Brooks
Penguin books
Second look

EH-U
Test tube
Legroom
Menu
Neptune
Festoon
Guess who
Wetsuit
Fresh fruit
Flesh wound
Nephew
Ted Hughes

Betty Boop
Wetherspoon
Twenty two

Rent a room
Leather shoes
Lemon juice
Lead balloon
Exit wound
Weatherproof
Crescent moon

EH-UH
Questlove
S Club
Step mum
Chestnuts
Bedbugs
Egg cup
Ketchup
Bread crumbed
Head butt
Death hunt
Hedge fund

Geoffrey Rush
Breakfast club
Flesh and blood
7-Up
Bendy Bus
Benelux

Feather touch
Leather gloves
Pension cuts

ER-A
Birthday
Wordplay
Survey
First aid
Earthquake
Birdcage
Work rate
Mermaid
Third base
Per se
Skirt steak

Kurt Cobain
Vernon Kaye
Purple Rain
Thirty eight
Murder rate
Circle Game
Vertebrae
Bird of prey
Percolate
Pearly gates

Curds and whey
Turn of phrase

ER-AH
Birdman
Third act
Lurpak
Work plan
First-hand
Dirt track
Burlap
Sperm bank
Nerve gas

Circus act
Bergerac
Bernie Mac
Burning man
Murder rap
Persian cat
Turning back
Workman's hat

ER-AR
Birdbath
First class

See ER-AH
Word art
Surcharge
Fur scarf
Churchyard
Birthmark
Birch bark

Working class
First to last
Circumstance
See ER-AH
Service charge
Work of art
Burger bar
Purple Heart

ER-AIR
Permed hair
Firmware

Circus bear
Curly haired
Stern but fair
Worse for wear

ER-E
Fir tree
Herpes
Bird seed
Worksheet
Turnkey
Search feed

Third degree
Hercules
Certainty
Mercury
Burgundy
Murder spree
Urgency
Herbal tea

ER-EH
WordPress
Perspex
Burnt ends
Hermes
Burlesque
Shirt dress
Bird's nest
Workbench
First leg

Bernadette
Turtleneck
Furry friends
Circumspect
Certain death
Birth defect
Perfect ten
Verbal threats
Percocet

ER-ER
Word search
Earthworm
Pervert
Work shirt
First serve
Curse word

Learning curve
Early bird
Circle jerk
Word for word

ER-EAR
First year
Worst fear
Third gear

Persevere
Thermosphere
Verge of tears

ER-I
Turnpike
Dirt bike
Termite
Stir-fry
Blurred lines
Birthright
Burns Night
Third eye
Curb side
Workshy
First prize

Circumscribe
Merchandise
Working nights
Furry dice
Dirty mind
Certified
Serpentine
Perfect skies

ER-IH
Wordsmith
Worshipped
Pursed lips
Worth it
Permit
Circuit
Work trip
First pick

Workmanship
Burger King
Percy Pig
Thirty six
Urban myth
German whip
Journalist

ER-O
Turbo
Bur oak
Workload
Turncoat
Word 'go'
Burnt toast
Peugeot

Dirt road
Merlot

Sherlock
    Holmes
Germophobe
Kurtis Blow
Vertigo
Work alone
Serpico
Burner phone
Nursing
    home

ER-OH
Sherlock
Birdwatch
Turn off
Workshop
Search box
Smirnoff
Word doc
Earth rod
Furlong
Curb stomp

Birkenstocks
30 Rock
Dirty dog
Worth a shot
Jürgen Klopp
Thermal socks
Wernham Hogg
Word of God
Burger box

ER-OR
Workforce
Surfboard
Turf wars
First born
Church doors
Dirt poor
Jerk sauce
Word score

Herbivore
Burger sauce
Murphy's Law
Thirty four
Jersey Shore

Perfect storm
Work abroad
Skirting board

ER-OW
Church mouse
Turndown
Earthbound
Burnout
Sperm count
Birdhouse

Jersey cow
Circus clown
Work it out
Turnaround
German hound
Word of mouth

ER-OI
Purloin
Turquoise
First choice
Sirloin
Dirk Kuyt

Jersey boys
Turning points

ER-OOH
First look
Sherwood
Workbook

Personhood

ER-U
Worm food
Curfew
Bird flu
Work boots
Church shoes

Persecute
Serving spoon
Curlicue
Servitude

ER-UH
Dirt truck
First blood
Nerf Gun
Turn up

Sperm duct
Surplus
Fur muff
Earth's crust

Persian rug
Murder one
Sherman Klump
Kirsten Dunst
Burger bun

EAR-A
Hearsay
Ear ache
Year 8
Tear stained
Beer crate

Hearing aid
Vera Drake
Here to stay
Clear as day

EAR-AH
Beer mat
Meerkat
Teargas

Earwax

Vera Wang

EAR-AR
Beer glass
See EAR-AH
Ear guards

Kierkegaard
Near and far
Here we are

EAR-AIR
Ear hair
Beer fair

Here and there

EAR-E
Cheerlead
Earpiece
Series
Theories

Dearie me!

EAR-EH
Near death
Beer keg
Deer head
Year 10
Smear test

Fear of death

EAR-ER
Ear worm

EAR-EAR
Pierced ear
Here, here
Steer clear

Tears for Fears
Years and Years

EAR-I
Near side
Hereby
Year 5
Clear skies
Queer Eye

Clear divide
Beer supply

EAR-IH
Near miss
Spearmint
Earrings
Herein
Gearshift
Earwig

EAR-O
Hero
Zero
Beer coat
Earlobe
Weirdo

Cheerio
Here we go

EAR-OH
Earshot
Fear not
Teardrop
Gearbox

Hereof
Veer off

Fear of God

EAR-OR
Rear door
Year four

Gears of War

EAR-OW
Clear out

Here and now
Hear me out

EAR-OI
Sheer joy
Spear point

Tears of joy

EAR-OOH	EAR-UH
Yearbook	Eardrum
	Year one
Period	Beer run
	Cheer up
EAR-U	Deer hunt
Rear view	Pierced tongue
Clear Blue	Clear cut
Hereto	Tear duct
Year 2	
	Clear as mud
Vera Cruz	Near enough
	Zero-sum

I-A
Mind games
Live Aid
Migraine
Ice age
Driveway
Crime wave
Nightshade
Typeface
Bike chain
Lightweight
Rice cake

Michael Caine
Pirate Bay
Cyberspace
5 a day
Bryan May
Cycle lane
Crying shame
Fireplace
Tidal wave

I-AH
Spice rack
Night cap
Right hand

Side-tracked
iPad
Hijacked
Mind map
Time lapse
Eyelash
Dry land

Pirate flag
Psychopath
Spider-Man
Iron clad
Wiretap
Tyra Banks
Final lap

I-AR
Pint glass
Eye mask
Flight path
See I-AH
Pie chart
Five star
Sidecar
Bright spark
Die hard
Fine art

Lifeguard
Hyde Park

Seismograph
Science class
Fibreglass
Cycle path
See I-AH
By and large
Irish guards
Rising star
Private parts
Tiger shark
Slide guitar
Tyre marks
Lion heart

I-AIR
White hair
Nike Airs
Nightmare
Fight fair
Highchair
Time's Square
Eyewear

Ryanair
Science fair
Flight of stairs
Lion's share
Spikey hair
Dining chair
Tyne and Wear

I-E
Pipe dreams
Spike Lee
ID
Ice cream
Sightsee
Thai Chi
Chai Tea
Livestream
Lime green
Crime scene
Timepiece

Driver's seat
Irony
Piracy
Siamese
Michael Sheen

Primal Scream
Time machine
Lima bean
Hide and seek
Bridal suite
Irish Sea

I-EH
Sidestep
Knife edge
White bread
Life vest
High tech
Nightdress
Mic check
Bike sheds
Mike Pence
Triceps
Mind-set

Simon Pegg
Side effects
Driving test
Fighter jet
Cyber sex
Skype address
Dialect

Tiger bread
Life and death

I-ER
Right turn
Sideburns
Christchurch
Kind words
Life's work
Wide berth
Iceberg
Price search

Fireworks
Bible verse
Fighting words
Private nurse
Wyatt Earp
Simon Bird
Heisenberg

I-EAR
Idea
Light year
Guy Pierce
My dear

Pioneer
Eyes and ears
Pint of beer
Biosphere
Dry your tears
Riot gear

I-I
Highlight
Nightlife
Bright side
Drive by
Lifelike
Pint size
White Stripes
Hindsight
Sci-fi
Prime time
Skydive

Firefly
Life of Pi
Ironside
Diatribe
Cyanide
Vital signs

Eye to eye
Ride or die

I-IH
Eyelid
Sidekick
Dry gin
Ice-pick
Light switch
High pitch
Night shift
Tight knit
Sky lit
Crisis

Lion King
Microchip
Pirate ship
Zionist
Wife and kids
Ryan Giggs
Tiger fish
Iron fist
Hieroglyph
Nihilist

I-O
Dido
Limestone
Lifeboats
Tightrope
Thigh bone
White oak
Pine cone
iPhone
Flight mode
Time zone
Sideshow

Idaho
Microphone
Michael Gove
Sly Stallone
Diet Coke
Quiet zone
Dial tone
Styrofoam
Dynamo
Isotope
Fire hose

I-OH
iPod
Crime watch
Cyclops
Whitewashed
Lifelong
Guide dog
Blind spot
Sight loss
Knife block
Livestock

Brighton Rock
Title Shot
Bio shock
Fire bombs
Michael Scott
Tie the knot
Writer's block
Lightning rod
Dialogues
Piping hot

I-OR
Side door
Eyesore
Sky Sports

High score
Guy Fawkes
Whiteboard
Crime lord
Life form
Psych ward
Light source
Cyborg

Sliding doors
Lightning storm
Dinosaur
Private law
Life support
Knife and fork
Pirate sword
Minotaur

I-OW
iCloud
Whitehouse
Eyebrows
Nightgown
Hideout
Lie down
Light brown
Live Lounge

China Town
Bridal gown
Pry around
Private grounds
Eiderdown
Lion's mouth
Ride it out
Lightning round

I-OI
Wide boy
Light soy
White noise
Thyroid
Knifepoint
Life buoy
Wise choice

Choirboy
Pride and joy
Biting point
Quiet voice

I-OOH
Right hook
Rhyme book
Knighthood

Plywood
Hind foot

Tiger Woods
Livelihood
Science book
Firewood

I-U
iTunes
Right move
IQ
Sky News
Haiku
Drive through
Typhoon
Ice cube
Bridegroom
Fine tuned
High noon
Dried fruit

Fireproof
Irish stew
Mighty Boosh
Irn Bru
Heidi Klum

Mining group
Writer's room
I am Groot
Ivan Ooze

I-UH
Fight club
Line up
Pine nut
Lifeblood
Light touch
Price cut
High jump
Bike pump
Night bus

Midas touch
Lighten up
Friar Tuck
Brian Clough
Cyberpunk
Ryder Cup
Fire truck
Driving gloves
Viaduct

IH-A
Brick lane
Nick Cave
King James
Shipshape
Inmate
Mixtape
Gift aid
Click bait
Fish cake
Rib cage
Ving Rhames

Prison break
Indicate
Cityscape
Figure skate
Fingerpaint
Jimmy Page
Give and take
Chick-fil-A
Picture frame
Imitate
Pillowcase

IH-AH	IH-AR	IH-AIR
Six pack	Hip flask	Ric Flair
Mismatch	Skin graft	Impair
Quicksand	Spin class	Swimwear
Chris Pratt	Slim fast	Thin air
Whiplash	Implants	Skincare
Gift wrapped	Witchcraft	Thick hair
Big Mac	*See IH-AH*	
Fish tank	Kick-start	Wicker chair
Pitch black	SIM card	Ginger hair
Wingman	Ming vase	Fitness wear
Bitch-slap	Fish farms	Disrepair
	Shipyard	Grizzly bear
Wicker man		
Instagram	Middle class	**IH-E**
Disneyland	*See IH-AH*	Mistreat
Riverbank	Jimmy Carr	Spring clean
Ginger snap	Cinema	Print screen
Piggy bank	Kwik-e-Mart	Lip read
Nickelback	Middle March	Pipsqueak
British Gas	Richmond Park	Chickpeas
Sycophant	Ringo Starr	Striptease
Tit-for-tat	Disembark	Whipped cream
Bric-a-brac	Scimitar	Trick knee
		Swiss cheese
		Displeased

Mr Bean
Chicken feed
Wisdom teeth
Christmas tree
Trilogy
Chimney sweep
Gift receipt
Bittersweet
Misery
Single cream
Figurine

IH-EH
Index
String vest
Misled
Windswept
Cliff edge
Shipwrecked
Big Ben
Pin head
Crib death
Distressed
6th Sense

50 cent
Cigarette

Internet
Silhouette
Mini-eggs
River Thames
Riz Ahmed
Chicken leg
Simply Red
Gingerbread

IH-ER
Intern
Big Bird
Ringworm
Inverse
Windsurf
Disperse
Midterms

Mr Burns
Miniskirt
Hindenburg
Friction burn
Chris de Burgh
Timberwork
Introvert
Twists and turns
Live and learn

Him and her
Interspersed
Single serve
Middle Earth

IH-EAR
Sincere
Pig's ear
King Lear
Mid-tier
Fifth Gear
Mishear

Insincere
Richard Gere
Britney Spears
Disappear
Crystal clear
Middle tier
Brigadier
Lincolnshire
Christmas cheer

IH-I
Midnight
Mince pie
Fistfight

Skin-tight
Windpipe
Flick knife
Big time
Pinstripe
Rip tide
King size

Lichtenstein
Mystify
Ginger Spice
District line
Chrissie Hynde
Pick your fights
Minimise
Stitch in time
Bridge of Spies
Chicken bites
Christmas lights
King and I
Chilli fries

IH-IH
Hit list
Chick flick
Pink slip
Lip stick

Cystic
Shindig
Pinprick
Slipped disc
Trick Trick
Slick Rick

Little Mix
Rizzle Kicks
Dixie Chicks
Fish and chips
Fingertips
Chicken strips
Fiddlesticks
Schindler's List
Physicist
Witnesses

IH-O
Intro
Big Show
Syndrome
Tiptoe
PIN code
Mink coat
Lymph nodes
Brimstone

Wishbone
Ring tone
Disrobe

Quincy Jones
Interscope
Video
Stick and poke
Chicken bone
Pigeon toed
Cicero
Pimlico
Indigo

IH-OH
Inbox
Tim Roth
Rick Ross
Lift-off
Chris Rock
Slingshot
King John
Gridlock
Wristwatch
Slipshod
Dishcloth

Chicken stock
Kicking off
Vic and Bob
British rock
Iggy Pop
Fingers crossed
Pixie Lott
Disney Shop

IH-OR
Rip Torn
In-laws
Vince Vaughan
Sixth form
Jigsaw
Switchboard
Pitchfork
King prawn
Fish course
Mint sauce
Shit-storm

Intercourse
Pinafore
Tipper Gore
Micky Rourke
Sixty four

Civil war
Winter sports

IH-OW
Whip-round
Midtown
Chris Brown
Print out
Inbound
Big mouth
Brick house
Pinned down

Mickey Mouse
Stick around
Chris O'Dowd
In and out
Simmer down

IH-OI
Sick boy
Disjoint
Midpoint
Invoice
Pink Floyd
Bitcoin
Chris Hoy

Illinois
Tipping point
Sigmund Freud
Little boy
Singing voice
Finger joint
Disappoint

IH-OOH
Driftwood
Fishhook
Tinned goods
Tim Cook
Big foot
Hymn book
Input
King's rook

Picture book
Inglenook
Chicken foot
Kindle wood
Mr Brooks
Sling your hook
In the hood
Bishop's crook
Simply put

IH-U	IH-UH
Tribute	Strip club
Issue	Nip/tuck
Fish food	In love
Igloo	Dim sum
Swimsuit	Mixed nuts
Pingu	Witch hunt
Tinned fruit	Mistrust
Wind proof	Fix up
Imbued	Kid gloves
In the loop	Nip and tuck
Interview	Liquid lunch
Switcheroo	Ginger nuts
Hitherto	Chicken run
Pick and choose	Sitting duck
Ginger root	Kitchen gloves
Wiggle room	Sippy cup
Chicken soup	
Citrus fruit	

O-A
Homebase
Stone Age
Showcase
Road rage
Throat ache
Opaque
Snowflake
Boatswain

Lower case
Poker face
Stowaway
Open day
Overstay
Motorcade
Trophy case
Ocean Spray
Novocaine
Blown away
Topher Grace

O-AH
Snowbank
Coke can
Jo Brand
Bromance

Slow Jams
Throat gland
Road map
Phone app
Throwback
Notepad
Clothes rack

Overlap
Yoga mat
Postman Pat
Poker hand
Lower back
Postage stamp

O-AR
Crowbar
Sonar
Co-star
Postcard
Go kart
Joe Hart
Faux pas
Flowchart
Coastguard
Blow dart
Ozark

Loan shark

Overdraft
See O-AH
Joan of Arc
Broken heart
Smoke alarm
Rosa Parks
Tony Stark
Joseph Kahn
Open bar
Coat of arms
Noah's ark
Côte d'Ivoire
Omaha

O-AIR
Au pair
Nowhere
Road flare
Sloane Square
Home share
Mohair

Polar Bear
Phone repair
Au contraire

Go Compare
Sofa chair
Tony Blair
Grosvenor
   Square
Open air
Baudelaire

O-E
Protein
Lowkey
Smokescreen
Goats cheese
Crow's feet
Roast beef
Motif
Oak tree
Showpiece

Dopamine
Oversleep
Loading screen
Rotary
Potency
Go between

Row of teeth
Open sea

O-EH
Stonehenge
Road test
Phone sex
Poached eggs
Grotesque
Codex
Code red
Tone deaf
Coke head

Motörhead
Overslept
Sofa bed
Polo neck
Soaking wet
Loaf of bread
No offence

O-ER
Auteur
Slow burn
Roadworks
Chauffeur

Growth spurt
Home turf
Snowbird
Loan word
Overt

Overworked
Sofa surf
Don't disturb
Kronenbourg
Spoken word
Open shirt
Rosenberg

O-EAR
No fear
Oh dear

Overhear
Coast is clear
Nowhere near
Close to tears
Cobra beer
Close your ears
Lower tier
Solar year

O-I
Home time
Co-sign
Strobe light
Stovepipe
Bow tie
Roadside
Coastline
Phone line
Blow dried
Lowlife
Snow White
Drone strike

Oversight
Closing time
Joseph Fiennes
Open mind
Motorbike
Poker site
Loaded dice
Coincide
Home and dry

O-IH
Road trip
Ghost ship

Rosehip
Glow stick
Post it
Homesick
Notice
Blowfish
Soap dish
Nose rings
Motive

Moby Dick
Motorist
Polar shift
Overfish
Showmanship
Roman myths
Chauvinist

O-O
Low blow
Soho
Fro comb
Snow globe
Postcode
Rowboat
Boatload

Go Pro
Stone's throw

Toby Jones
Holy Ghost
Comatose
Overdose
Rodeo
Home alone
Chromosome
Go for broke
Vocal coach
Homophobe
Post Malone

O-OH
Phone box
Robot
Show off
Clothes shop
Roadblock
Botox
Post op
Snowdrop
Ghost Dog

Open top
Robocop
Soda pop
Pros and cons
Rogan Josh
Voting bloc
Photoshop
Overwatch

O-OR
Cohorts
Snowboard
Clothes horse
Blowtorch
Mohawk
Phone cord

Trojan horse
Overboard
Motorsports
Solar storm
Coping saw
No remorse
Vocal cords
Local haunt

O-OW
Motown
Home crowd
Throw down
Snow plough
Ghost house
Know-how

Motor-mouth
Overground
Broken down
Poke around
Homeward
    bound
Holy cow
Know the crowd
Open house

O-OI
Homeboy
Pro-choice
Phone voice
No joy
Low point
Grosse Pointe

Polaroid
Tone of voice
Overjoyed
Sophie's Choice
Focal point
Poster boy
Opioid

O-OOH
Oakwood
Notebook
Coat hook
Rose bush
No good
Slow-cooked

Closer look
Overcooked
Open book

O-U
Home truths
O2
Phone booth
Cloakroom
Tofu

Show tune
Stone fruit
Boat shoes

Jonas Blue
Focus group
Overdue
Opal fruits
Chosen few
Local news
Sober truth
Photo booth

O-UH
Doughnut
Grown ups
Rogue One
Home front
Soap suds
Show jump
Blowgun
Tow truck
Rosebud

Coconut
Motor truck
Open up

Smoking gun
Logan's Run
Poking fun
Rowing club
Local pub

OH-A
Prostate
Prom date
John Wayne
Tom Waits
Shockwave
Wrong way
Hot cakes
Bobsleigh
Concaved
Off-day

Mockingjay
Bolognese
Stock exchange
Complicate
John McClane
Pocket change
Commonplace
Dr Dre
Doris Day

Lost in Space
Orangeade

OH-AH
Top hat
WhatsApp
Jockstrap
Contract
Dog tag
Tom Hanks
John Ham
Wash rag
Oxfam
Hot tap
Stop gap
Crosshatched

Copycat
Polymath
Bottle cap
Johnny Cash
Shopping bag
Pontefract
Colin Hanks
Stocking cap

OH-AR

Podcast
Shot glass
Top class
Pot plants
Contrast
See OH-AH
Scotchgard
Montage
Pop chart
John Barnes
Rock star
Squad car
En garde
Bombard
Dockyard

Song and dance
Robert Plant
Olive branch
See OH-AH
Shopping cart
Bodyguard
Johnny Marr
Promenade
Chocolate bar
Oligarch

OH-AIR

Software
Crosshairs
Compere
Con Air
Dog hair
Job fair
Pom Bears
Bomb scare

Rocking chair
Solitaire
Stop and stare
Body hair
Bon Iver
Stocks and
   shares
Fozzie Bear
Foster care

OH-E

Hot seat
John Cleese
Swat team
Dog breed
Crossbeam
Off key

Proxy
Shop keep
Mob Deep
Top speed

Coral reef
Logger's Leap
Socrates
Colony
Coffee bean
Lock and key
Pot of tea
Constantine
Cottage cheese
Morrissey

OH-EH

Scotch egg
Loch Ness
Hotbed
Ross Kemp
Frogs legs
John West
Drop dead
Complex
Context
Bomb threat

Common sense
On the fence
Rotten eggs
Loggerheads
Johnny Depp
Foreign Press
Consequence
Sausage fest
Bottleneck
Olive bread

OH-ER
Songbird
Wrong turn
Converse
Clockwork
Watchword
Nocturne
Mossberg
Long term
John Hurt
Job search
Dog fur

Stop and search
Watch and
    learn

Colin Firth
Olly Murrs
Mockingbird
Kopparberg
Donkeywork
Robert Burns

OH-EAR
Dog years
Popped ears
Top Gear
Shropshire

Volunteer
Commandeer
Donkey's years
Foster's Beer
Bottom tier
Boromir
Oxfordshire
Block your ears

OH-I
Frostbite
Posh Spice
Clockwise
Fog lights

Crossed eyes
Bonsai
Hog tied
Bomb site
Stop sign
Botfly
Oxide

Robin Wright
Spotify
Colonised
Boxercise
What's the
    time?
Boris Bikes
Compromise
Concubine
Vodka lime
Cottage pie

OH-IH
Chopsticks
Offspring
Gosling
Log in
Pop quiz
Toxic

Cross stitch
Dogfish
Softmints
Oxbridge
Shoplift

Shopping list
Hockey sticks
Optimist
Floppy disk
Orifice
Chocolate kiss
Rotten fish
Comic strip
Obelisk
Robin Thicke

OH-O
Trombone
Tom Jones
Bongos
Longboat
Cockroach
Bob Hope
John Snow
Joss Stone
Rob Lowe

Crossbow
Combo
Topcoat

John Torode
Monaco
Horoscope
On the nose
Collarbone
Foster home
Dominoes
Colin Jost

OH-OH
Romcom
Watchdog
Hotshot
Hopscotch
Topshop
Odd socks
Long johns
Crop top

Ocelot
Coffee pot
Chopping block
Sausage dog

Monologue
Body Shop
Pocket watch
Chocolate log
Gogglebox

OH-OR
Concord
Popcorn
Onslaught
Washboard
Frogspawn
Top drawer
Hot sauce
Encore

Roger Moore
Hover board
Chopping
    board
Croque
    monsieur
God of War
Tomahawk
Cosmonaut
Rocky IV
Bottom floor

Rocking horse
Horrorcore

OH-OW
Locked out
Moscow
Foxhound
Bogged down
Lost count
Doghouse
Washout
Compound

Lost and found
Cottonmouth
Coffeehouse
On the town
Common
    ground
Body count
Boxing bout
Knock around

OH-OI
Convoy
Tomboy
Cod loin

Dog toy
Bok Choi
Rob Roy
John Voight
Hotpoint
Conjoined

Lobby boy
Tonka toy
What's the
    point?
Lost your voice?
Copper coins

OH-OOH
Monmouth
Dogwood
Songbook
Godhood

Pocketbook
Hollywood
Thomas Cook
Robin Hood
Oxford Brookes
Jolly good
Knock on wood

Dr Hook
Octopus

OH-U
Pontoon
Tom Cruise
Jon Woo
Stockroom
Monsoon
Hot soup
Pop group
Log flume
Fox News
Dog food
Bombproof

Orange juice
Prostitute
Sonic Youth
Motley Crue
Montagues
Dr Who
Hostel II
Gospel truth
Solitude
Hot pursuit

OH-UH	OR-A	Horseback
Top Trumps	Cornflakes	Format
John Donne	Norway	Doormat
Washtub	Poor taste	Floor plan
Crosscut	Portrait	Launch pad
Foxglove	Doorframe	Thorax
Conduct	Horse race	Sports bag
Clogged plug	Short-changed	
Hot Fuzz	Foreplay	Quarterback
Yacht club	Court date	Borderland
Dogs Trust	Broadway	Gordon Banks
Soft touch	War paint	Torture rack
Long jump		Sorting Hat
Rock club	Watergate	Laundromat
Godson	Port of Spain	Force your hand
	Norman Bates	Corner flag
Donald Duck	Storage space	Courtesan
Konnie Huq	Born and raised	
Forrest Gump	Mortgage rates	**OR-AR**
Boxing gloves	Walk of shame	Warpath
Washing up	Fornicate	Forecast
Pocket fluff	Born again	Rorschach
Bottom rung		*See OR-AH*
Coffee cup	**OR-AH**	Pornstar
Hockey puck	Broadband	Forearm
	Shorthand	Sports bra
	Straw hat	Courtyard

Store card
Corn-starch
Floor staff

Tour de France
Autograph
Boarding pass
See OR-AH
Watermark
Horse and cart

OR-AIR
Horsehair
Forebear
Warfare
Sportswear
Foursquare
Lord's Prayer
Lawn chair

Auburn hair
Gorgon stare
Corner chair
Formal wear
Thoughts and
    prayers

OR-E
Northeast
Born free
Door key
Corned beef
Sean Bean
Foresee
Pork cheek
Horse breed
Broadsheets

War and Peace
Dawson's Creek
Forty three
Normandy
Portuguese
Chalk and
    cheese
Water-ski
Autumn leaves
Yorkshire tea

OR-EH
Corn fed
Doorstep
Dawn French
George Best

Northwest
Sean Penn
Vortex
Warheads
Shortbread
Launderette

Portishead
Cause of death
More or less
Corner desk
Hornet's nest
Watershed
Walking dead

OR-ER
Coursework
George Burns
Store clerk
Broadchurch
Foreword
Law firm
Short term

Thora Hird

OR-EAR
Warm beer
Sports gear
Yorkshire
George Weah

Auctioneer
Cornish Beer
Bored to tears

OR-I
Tour guide
Hawkeye
Porn site
Fortnight
War cry
Horsefly
Pork pie
Jawline
Rawhide
Sword fight

Porcupine
Porky pies
Lord alive
Fortified
Story time

Organise
Water slide
Short supply
Sporty Spice
Warning signs
Tourist guide

OR-IH
Nordic
Caustic
Drawbridge
Forklift
Lordship
Shortlist
War Pigs
Swordfish
Sports drink

Sportsmanship
Organist
Walking stick
Corner kick
Talking shit
Caught a
    glimpse
Dorsal fin
Forty winks

OR-O
Wardrobe
Torso
Morse code
Sore throat
Forego
Bordeaux
Sean Combs
Jawbone
Corn rows
Porno

Warner Bros
Audio
Cornerstone
Scorpio
Oreo
Horny toad
Morning show
War at home

OR-OH
Fort Knox
Pawn shop
Warlock
Pork chops
Straw Dogs

Schwarzkopf
Sore spot
Warthog
War god
Doorknob

Courtney Cox
Orthodox
Gorbachev
Corner shop
Storage box
Northern Rock
Waterlogged
Cordoned off

OR-OR
Warlord
Broadsword
4 door
Floorboards
Forlorn
Store-bought
Forecourt
Warsaw
Short straw
Cork board

Water sports
Force majeure
Smorgasbord
Court of law
Yorkshire Moors
Pause for
    thought
Door to door
Port to port
Storyboard
Geordie Shore
Por favor

OR-OW
Worn down
Courthouse
Foreground
Dormouse
Storm cloud

Gordon Brown
Haunted house
Morning gown
Forty ounce
Bordertown
Horse and
    Hound

Quarter pound
Watered down
North and
    South

OR-OI
Sore point
Pork loin

Corduroy
Water Boy
Talking point
Orgazoid

OR-OOH
Forefoot
Bournemouth
Awkward
Law book

Storybook

OR-U
Corfu
Storm proof
Horseshoe
Fortune

War wound
Storerooms
Foredoomed
Corkscrew

Portaloo
Sorting room
Quarter to
Waterproof
Morning dew
Fortitude
Auto-tune
Mortal wound

OR-UH
Tour bus
Shortcut
Warm up
Sawdust
Awestruck
Sports club
George Stubbs

Courtney Love
All-in-one
Morning sun

OW-A
Outrage
Downplayed
Chow mein
Housemate
Sound waves
Vouchsafe
Southgate

Cow and Gate
Power play
Outer space
Sour grapes
Out of place
Shower tray
Mountain lake
House of Pain

OW-AH
Mouse trap
Cowpat
Southbank
Outback
House cat
Poundland
Soundtrack

Shouting match
Down the hatch
Sour Patch
Shower cap
Bound and
    gagged
Power nap
House of Wax
Counteract
Rounders bat

OW-AR
OutKast
Houseplant
Stout glass
Downdraft
See OW-AH
South Park
Mouth guard
Clown car
Round arch
Sound bar
Cow shark
Lounge bar

Power plant
Shower bath

Hourglass
Mountain pass
See OW-AH
House of cards
Out of charge

OW-AIR
Brown bear
Downstairs
Loungewear
Out there
Town fair
House share

County fair
Mousey hair

OW-E
House key
Southeast
Mouthpiece
Downbeat
Rowntree
Bounty

Downing Street
Flower seeds
Cowardly

Sound asleep
Sour cream
Counting sheep
Mountain peak
Shower scene
Out of reach

OW-EH
Roundheads
Southwest
Brown bread
Bounced
    cheque
Sound test
Outstretched
Cowshed

Sound effects
Fountain pen
Now and then
Round the bend
Out of breath
Pound of flesh
Trouser press
Flower bed
Shower head
House arrest

OW-ER
Outburst
Housework
Brown Shirts
Crowd surf

Down to earth
Power surge
Howard Stern
Powder burns
Out of turn

OW-EAR
Stout beer
Sound gear

Out of here
Mountaineer
Sour beer
Loud and clear
House of Fear
Thousand years

OW-I
Outshine
Downtime
Housewives

South side
Sound bite
Round-eyed
Cowhide
Brown rice

Mountain bike
Out of time
Down the line
Power slide
Sound advice

OW-IH
Outfit
Round trip
Township
Auschwitz
Cow's lick
Downswing

Out of it
Power trip
Tower Bridge
Trouser zip
Counterfeit

OW-O
Download
Outgrow
Houseboat
Brown nose

Mountain goat
Counting crows
House and home
Down the road
Sourdough
Power hose

OW-OH
Outfox
Sound off
Pound shop
Mouthwash
Hound dog
Groundhog
Cowpox

Flowerpot
Mountaintop
Out of stock
Tower block
Sour pops

Round the clock
Power wash
Frowned upon
Mouthing off

OW-OR
Southpaw
Downpour
Ground floor
Crown Court
Outdoor
Crowdsourced
Soundboard
Brown sauce

Sounding board
Crown of thorns
House of Lords
Out of sorts
Power chord

OW-OW
SoundCloud
Countdown
Outbound
Chow Chow
Townhouse

Bow wow
Loudmouth
Southbound
House proud

Out and out
Powerhouse
Sauerkraut
Council house
Roundabout
Mountain town

OW-OI
Loud noise
Cowboy
Pound coin
Out-voice
South Point

Brownie points
Out of joint
PowerPoint

OW-OOH
Output

Sourpuss

OW-U
How to
Outdo
Soundproof
Ground loop
Clown shoes
Mount doom
Scout group

Howard Hughes
Showerproof
Powder room
Power through
Mountain Dew
Out the blue
Sour fruits

OW-UH
Outcome
Groundnut
Mouse hunt
Scout hut
Crowd fund
Round up

Power cut
Out of luck

Powder puff
Hounds of Love
Flower bud
Trouser cuffs

OI-A
Oy vey
Point Break
Toy train
Joint pain
Coin tray
Soy glaze
Noise gate
Foyer

Coin a phrase
Toilet break

OI-AH
Boy band
Lloyd's bank
Point blank
Deutschland
Join hands
Lloyd Banks

Join the ranks

OI-AR
Foy Vance
See OI-AH
Point guard
Toy car
Koi carp
Coin star

Boyish charm
Poison darts
Oyster card
Royal guard

OI-AIR
Toy fair
Joint care
Boyswear

Joint repair

OI-E
Roy Keane
Soybean
Noisey

Soya bean
Goya seed

Joinery
Buoyancy
Toilet seat
Loyalty
Soylent Green
Joining fee

OI-EH
Toy chest
Boyfriend

Boyz II Men
Poison pen
Boiled egg

OI-ER
Voyeur
Cruyff Turn
Coin purse
Joint work

OI-EAR

OI-I
Joyride
Muay Thai
Toylike

Point device
Moisturise

OI-IH
Joystick
Coin flip

Royal mint
Loyalist

OI-O
Toy-boat
Boyzone
Voice note

Poison oak

OI-OH
Loincloth
Toy shop
Boycott
Voice box
Coydog

Boying off

OI-OR
Boy George
Soy sauce
Toy swords

Toilet doors
Buoyant force
Troy McClure
Royal Courts
Groin support
Oil war
Spoilsport
Hoisin sauce
Join the cause

OI-OW
Toy Town
Boy Scout

Joint account

OI-OI
Oi-Oi
Toy-boy

Hoi polloi
Boiling point

OI-OOH
Boyhood

OI-U
Boy blue

Royal Blue
Poison root
Point of view
Boiler room

OI-UH
Roy Hudd
Toy gun
Joined up
Coin cup
Soy nut

Royal flush
Toilet brush
Toys R Us
Join the club
Poisoned cup
Lawyer-up
Hoisin duck

OOH-A
Wood grain
Bookcase
Footrace
Soot stains

Wooden stake
Sugarcane

OOH-AH
Foot rash
Book stack
Bushwhack
Pushback
Good man

Pudding can
Wooden hand
Cookie stand
Pussy cat

OOH-AR
Hood pass
See OOH-AH
Bookmark
Foot spa

Hook bra
Chutzpah

Cooking class
Looking glass
See OOH-AH
Cookie jar
Boulevard
Push-up bra

OOH-AIR
Book fair
Footwear
Pushchair
Cookware

Wooden chair

OOH-E
Look-see
Footsie
Good grief
Woodley

Sugar free
Booking fee

Booker T
Crooked teeth

OOH-EH
Bookends
Footsteps
Woodshed
Good stead
Cooked egg

Wooden leg
Bucharest

OOH-ER
Woodwork
Hookworm

OOH-EAR
Goodyear
Footgear

Looky here
Worcestershire

OOH-I
Goodbye
Suge Knight

Woodlice
Footlights
Cooked rice
Brookside
Pushbike
McFly

Sugar pie
Good advice
Lookalike
Booker Prize
Took your time
Crooked I
Cooking light
Womanize
Book of Life

OOH-IH
Wood chips
Footbridge
Hoodwinked
Woodwind

Bulletin
Cookie mix
Wooden stick

OOH-O
Punto
Footnote
Good show
Hook nose
Cook stove

Sugarloaf
Wooden boat
Cooking show
Cookie dough

OOH-OH
Woodstock
Bookshop
Good God
Push pop
Cook off
Bush frog

Cooking pot
Woolly sock

OOH-OR
Good lord
Wood saw

Footsore
Book launch

Wooden horse
Cooking course

OOH-OW
Lookout
Woodlouse
Put down

Wooden house
Foot and mouth

OOH-OI
Footboy
Good point

Wooden toy

OOH-OOH
Cookbook
Goodwood
Couscous

Cook the books
Looking good
Sugar bush

OOH-U
Footloose
Good news
Cuckoo
Wood glue

Puss in Boots
Wooden spoon
Lookie-loo
Boogaloo
Good as new
Whoop-di-doo
Bulletproof
Sugar cube

OOH-UH
Push up
Book club
Shook Ones
Good luck
Wood duck
Foot rub

Looking up
Pudding cup
Sugar lump

U-A
Shoelace
New age
Roommate
Loose change
Toothpaste
Fruitcake
Doomsday
Suitcase
Bruce Wayne
Food chain

Lucozade
Rue the day
Music taste
User base
Ruminate
Nutrigrain
Shooting pains
Super 8
Human race

U-AH
Tube map
Tupac
Boom bap
Gulag

Fruit bat
Do-rag
Flu jab
Blu tack

Superbad
Music act
Student flat
Ruby Wax
Uber app
Scoobie snack
Hoover Dam
Booby trap
Chew the fat
Google Maps

U-AR
Bluegrass
Newscast
Moondance
Hugh Grant
Fused glass
See U-AH
Rhubarb
Fubar
Hoopla
Roulade

Used cars
Doodah

Supercharge
Shooting star
Bruno Mars
Blues guitar
Music charts
Student card
Fuselage
Oohs and ahs
Coup d'etat
Beauty mark

U-AIR
Moon bear
Who cares?
Two pair
Root hair

Pubic hair
Truth or dare
Student fair
Shoe repair
Lumière
Rupert Bear
Uber fare

U-E	U-EH	U-ER
Boutique	Crew neck	Usurped
Lou Reed	Poop deck	Superb
Bruce Lee	Sous-chef	Bluebird
Routine	Goose step	Rude words
Moonbeam	Spoon fed	Truth hurts
News team	Moose head	Juice Burst
Proofread	Bootleg	Oo-er
Loose leaf	Duplex	Runeberg
Tout suite	Roulette	U-turn
Groom's speech	Group text	
Blue cheese	Due west	Google Earth
		Universe
Stewart Lee	Judi Dench	Uber surge
Super freak	Unicef	Lose your nerve
Mutant gene	Sudafed	Fruit preserve
Losing streak	Fruit and veg	Student nurse
Nudist beach	Future tense	Do your worst
Judas Priest	Unisex	
Duty free	Toothpick test	**U-EAR**
Human League	Music tech	Root beer
Lucid dream	Use your head	New year
Ulysses	Rooms to rent	Bluebeard
Beauty queen	Student debt	
Booster seat	Truth in jest	Souvenirs
Fruit machine		Lumineers
		Scuba gear

Human ear
Pruning shears
Stuart Pearce
Mutineer
Fusilier

U-I
Due time
Newsnight
Tube strikes
Food fight
Fruit pie
Moonlight
QI
Brunei
Shoeshine
Blue skies
True lies

Supersized
Suicide
Cutie pie
Do or die
Euthanise
Music night
Suit and tie
Crucify

Google Drive
Junior high
Food supply
Human rights
Losing side

U-IH
Loose fit
Toothpick
Broomstick
Cue tip
Blueprint
Moonlit
Shoestring
Cupid
Hubris
Stupid
Cruise ship
Bootlick

Crucifix
Lunatic
Music biz
Fugitive
Tuna fish
Rupert Grint
Humanist

Music quiz
Super quick

U-O
Sumo
Tombstone
News show
Glucose
Room tone
Cluedo
Ruth Jones
Group home
U-boat
Blue note
Shoe Zone
Fruit loaf

UFO
Student loan
Yu-gi-oh
Truman Show
Studio
Tudor Rose
Human clone
Cupid's bow
Google Chrome

U-OH
Tube sock
Dew drop
Boondocks
Stew pot
Boombox
Snoop Dogg
Shoe shop
Rooftop
June Lodge
Boob job
Coupons

Beauty spot
Rubicon
Whooping
    cough
Music box
Superhot
Hugo Boss
Duologue
Snooker shot
Student job

U-OR
Brute force
Jude Law

Lukewarm
Newborn
Mood board
Root cause
Tuborg
Shoehorn
New York

Uniform
Human Torch
Unicorn
Susan Storm
Music tour
You and yours
Food for
    thought
News report

U-OW
Newfound
Due south
Shootout
Boom Town
Luau
Lose count

Proving grounds
Do the rounds
Moving out
Student house
Root around
Luton Town
Tudor Crown
Rufus Hound

U-OI
Rude boy
Viewpoint
Cuboid
Chew toy

Lucian Freud
Lose your
    voice?
Prove a point
Humanoid
Rheumatoid

U-OOH
New look
Sue Cook

U-U
YouTube
Soup spoon
U2
Boob tube
Fruit juice
Voodoo
Bluetooth
Who's Who
Booze cruise
Newsroom

Lucy Liu
Scooby Doo
Doom and
    gloom
Futureproof
Rubik's Cube
Superfoods

U-UH
True love
Moonstruck
Crew cut
Fruit cup
Toothbrush
Dune bug

Goosebumps
Glue gun

Superdrug
Fruit and nut
Chewing gum
Loosen up
Movie buff
Lose your touch

UH-A
Monday
Rump steak
Nutcase
Cupcake
Sunbathe
Bus lane
One way
Bug spray
Lunch break
Update
Front page
Duct tape
Runway
Floodgates
Bloodstained

Drum'n'bass
Russell Kane
Up-to-date
Fun and games
Stomach ache
Runaway
Come of age
Mother's day
Hurricane
Upper case
Underway

UH-AH
Suntan
Comeback
Love shack
Scumbag
Dunce hat
Hubcap
Dustpan
Mud flap
Grudge match
Pub snack
Thumbtack
Blood bank

Rubber band
Russell Brand
Motherland
Understand
Punching bag
Jumping jacks
Muscle cramp
Running track
Honey trap
Lumberjack
Thunder crack
Bucket hat

UH-AR
Sundance
Stuck fast
Bloodbath
Bus pass
See UH-AH
Jump start
Stunt car
Tongue bar
Sub-par
Love heart
Junk yard
Club card

Upper class
Bubble bath
Public path
Russell Grant
Underpass
See UH-AH
Come to harm
Muscle car
Colour chart
Lucky stars
Wonderbra

UH-AIR
Unfair
Sun bear
Somewhere
Upstairs
Funfair
Club chair
Bugbear
Rush Hair
Bus fare

Mothercare
Thoroughfare
Underwear
Love affair

Bucket chair
Double dare
Tupperware
Russell Square
Unprepared
Tough but fair
Russian Bear

UH-E
Bus seat
Blood stream
Duckweed
Unseen
Gumtree
Lunch meat
Rugby
Sun cream
One piece
Buckwheat

Double cream
Submarine
Underneath
Dungarees
Comfort eat
Subtlety
Cup of tea

Colour scheme
Brush your
    teeth
Tongue in cheek
Gum disease
Surrey Quays

UH-EH
Bunk bed
Subtext
Unstressed
Blood test
Upset
Plug head
Nutmeg

Suffragettes
Runny eggs
Public sex
Rubberneck
Cutting edge
London Met
Dunderhead
Underwent
Number 10
Monkey wrench
Sudden death

Double bed
Cover text

UH-ER
Unstirred
Upturned
Sunburst
Dunkirk
Submerged
Come first
Young Turks
Buzzword
Rug burns
Bloodthirst
Lovebirds

Undeserved
Underworked
Hummingbird
Mother Earth
Just desserts
Zuckerberg
Other words
Lunch and learn
Public works

UH-EAR
Unclear
Duff Beer
Frontier

Buccaneer
Musketeers
Hunting gear
Chugging beer
Scruffy beard
Once a year
Puppeteer
Floods of tears
Understeer
Public sphere

UH-I
Sunshine
Lunchtime
Punch line
Mud-fight
Tongue tied
Love life
Bus ride
Blood type
Plum pie
Unkind

Uptight
Dust mite
Stunt bike

Hunger strike
Underlined
Monetised
Otherwise
Summertime
Hunting knife
Butterfly
Guttersnipe
Humble pie
London Eye
Countryside
Subdivide

UH-IH
Upwind
Lovesick
Sunkissed
Public
Unstitched
Drumsticks
Gunships
Thumbprint
Bucks Fizz

Pub quiz
Monkfish
Front flip

Sonny Jim
Mothership
Cuttlefish
Lover's tiff
Upper lip
Butterkist
London Bridge
Publicist
Rubbish tip

UH-O
Front row
Sunstroke
Blood soaked
Cut-throat
Upload
Love note
Unknown
Umbro
Jump-rope
Tugboat
Touchstone

Undergrowth
Russell Crowe
Bungalow
Mother lode
Pumice stone
Touch and go
Funny bone
Rum and Coke
Puppet show
Undisclosed
Comfort zone
Running joke
Honeycomb

UH-OH
Sunspots
One stop
Dunlop
Gum drop
Junk shop
Blood clot
Somewhat
Jump shot
Unlocked
Glovebox
Love songs
Gunshot

Punk rock
Subplot

Russell Hobbs
Jungle rot
Butterscotch
Money shot
Puppy dog
Honeypot
Double crossed
Cutting costs
Touching cloth
Bunny hop
Summer job
Hunter's lodge

UH-OR
Unsure
Done for
Drug store
Uproar
Slumlord
Front door
Rushmore
Blood sport
Thumb war

Tug of war
Motherboard
Juggernaut
Underscore
Thunderstorm
Monkey paw
Uninsured
Public law
Summer shorts

UH-OW
Sundown
Unwound
Kung Pow
Cub scouts
Clubhouse
Dust cloud
Somehow
Dugout
Tough crowd

London Town
Underground
Up and down
Summerhouse
Runaround
Mother Brown

Thundercloud
Hunting
    grounds

UH-OI
Lovejoy
Busboy
Gunpoint
Unvoiced
Subjoin
Stuffed toy

Jump for joy
Null and void
Unemployed
Lucky coin
Mummy's boy
Cuddly toy

UH-OOH
Touch wood
Uncooked
Front foot
Jump hook
Stud book

Jungle Book
Oven cooked
Understood
Ruste Juxx
Brotherhood
London look
Hungerford

UH-U
Front room
Sunroof
Junk food
Gun-proof
Mushroom
Ugg boots
Duck Soup
Kung Fu
Untrue
Blood moon

Jumpsuit
Uproot
Bucktooth

Buckaroo
London zoo
Function room
Mother Goose
Douglas Booth
Underuse
Comfort food
Honeydew
W
Rugby boots

UH-UH
Undone
Punch drunk
Love-struck

Fun run
Buzz cut
Someone
Stun gun
Stuck up
Dump truck
Tough luck
Bloodlust

Buttercup
Upper crust
Thunderstruck
Rubber duck
Double Dutch
Sucker-punch
Honeybuns
Undercut
Bubble butt
Puppy love

Index

Lightning Source UK Ltd.
Milton Keynes UK
UKHW021656120821
388690UK00007B/322

9 781786 236685